ESSENTIAL POETS SERIES 170

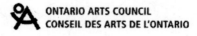

Canada Council   Conseil des Arts
for the Arts   du Canada

ONTARIO ARTS COUNCIL
CONSEIL DES ARTS DE L'ONTARIO

Guernica Editions Inc. acknowledges the support of
the Canada Council for the Arts and the Ontario Arts Council.
The Ontario Arts Council is an agency of the Government of Ontario.

JIM CHRISTY

MARIMBA FOREVER

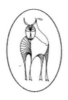

GUERNICA
TORONTO–BUFFALO–LANCASTER (U.K.)
2010

Antonio D'Alfonso, editor
Guernica Editions Inc.
P.O. Box 117, Station P, Toronto (ON), Canada M5S 2S6
2250 Military Road, Tonawanda, N.Y. 14150-6000 U.S.A.

Distributors:
University of Toronto Press Distribution,
5201 Dufferin Street, Toronto (ON), Canada M3H 5T8
Gazelle Book Services, White Cross Mills, High Town, Lancaster LA1 4XS U.K.

Typeset by Selina in Palatino 10/13.
First edition.
Printed in Canada.

Legal Deposit – Third Quarter
Library of Congress Catalog Card Number: 2010925333
Library and Archives Canada Cataloguing in Publication
Christy, Jim, 1945-
Marimba forever / Jim Christy.
(Essential poets series ; 170)
Poems.
ISBN 978-1-55071-316-9
I. Title. II. Series: Essential poets series ; 170.
PS8555.H74M37 2010   C811'.54   C2010-904745-1

CONTENTS

5

DRESSED FOR BUSINESS

I saw her reflection
In the window of the dollar store,
A ghostly beauty between
Sponge mops and plastic swords
Above a sated Mary
And a sad-eyed man
From Nazareth.
I turned, and she half-smiled
But backed at my approach,
A young woman dressed
For business. I went on
My way, hearing her behind
In metronome heels, glimpsing
Her in windows like a good
Private eye. I turned
Again. She smiled again.
Pale skin, and dark eyes
Like black headlights
Of a white car in the snow. What
Did that look signify? Maybe
I know what it might have meant
Not all that many years ago. So
I walked and stopped, and she
Did the same, like a couple
Of windup toys. And in
Another window: electronic
Stuff I neither need nor
Understand, her there
Behind me, and I asked
"What is it?"
She shivered or maybe I want

To think she shivered, like
A pony. "Do we know each
Other?" And again the slit
Of a smile as if the sun peeked
Over the ridge before thinking
Better of it. She nodded then
And headed for the College car.
I saw it take her away
West, the beautiful young
Woman watching
Me from the window.

JIMINY CRICKET

He could be the world's oldest dope fiend leaning
Against the lamppost at Hollywood and Vine – Pep
Boys' amp and speaker, Les Paul purloined
Knockoff – like something
That didn't change after Halloween
And tell the kiddies he
Was only kidding – playing blues.

"See the old dude? Escaped from the indigent
Old entertainers' home," said Fat Maurice,
Resident know-it-all, Mr. Smarty Pants
Of the lobby Morris Chair that evening
Sometime in the early 1970s. "That
There old vampire invented scat singing,
Cut the first jazz vocal, was a singing cowboy,
Is even in the goddamned ukulele hall
Of fame. He earned millions, boy. Millions.
And he still wound up with an up-turned
Fedora at his feet."

And the fat man smiles, glad to offer
Even more evidence that the game
Is rigged and Fate's a mother,
Which he's known all along, of course,
And which is why he never even played
The game.

Meanwhile, the cadaver on the corner, veteran
Of six wives and as many addictions, 147
Films and 749 recordings, bends a note
Long enough to nab the flask from a cave

Inside his sports coat, and leans
His head back. You think his conk's
Going to snap off and roll
All the way down the junkie street
To Frederick's – old white man, white
Whiskers on chicken neck. "Aahh! Lord,"
He says, making six notes of it
As he stares at the stars, wishing,
Because like Fat Maurice said, it
Makes no difference who
You are.

THREE A.M. IN NO MAN'S LAND

This is the realm of shortdogs and mouse
Hours. Would that the daylight were
More distant than Danebola.

All the rock
And rollers hug their blankets and dream
Their tunes in TV ads.

They're scant few of us about,
Conscripts all and scattered like stardust.
We dine in the void, cover the water
Front and fish the Sargasso Sea.

A fellow's by a shortwave
Near Arctic Red River and outside
His cabin the black ice cracks
Like snapping 78s, while Brew Moore
Plays along.

That woman
Up all night in Monaco has
An emptiness deeper
Than any casino.

We recognize each other as sure
As if camp guards tattooed
Lady Day's gardenia on our forearms.
We slink down Perdido Street, and keys
Like comets fall from upper
Windows. They're wrapped
In notes full of promises destined

Never to be redeemed.

The sound track to this b-movie
Is an all night show from 1938 – here
It's always 1938 – and we listen while
Some crazy little vegetarian tears up
The Munich Pact. But we prevail;
Lester's still our leader.

It's the No Man's Land of three A.M.
Crows peck at forms crucified on the wire.
Our souvenirs are not Lugers
But discarded illusions

On we slog, down
The up escalator of the coming
Daylight. A mouse hours' army
Bidding the call
Of the muted trumpets
And the tenor saxophones.

DELAWARE AVENUE

Back on Delaware Avenue, thirty-six
Years later, no wiser
But closer to the subway.
Went around the world six
Times to get to the other
Side of the street. Midnight,
The moonlight's like melted
Silver on kids' swing set.
TV antennas make skeletons
Against the black sky.
There's a cat paw trail
Across the shed roof snow and
Art Tatum's by my side
Playing on an invention
That wasn't around back
Then, a memory at
The tip of every furious finger:
The Montevideo refugee, the
Third-floor handwritten novel,
Junk store camera on wooden
Chair aimed at black and white
Moonwalk, house a fug of pot
Smoke when the Mountie called,
Sniffed and grinned in the vestibule,
The landlord's ex-wife on
The chesterfield, full skirt
Over her head, sprawled
In drunk sleep like
A crime scene torso, hand

In hand with the famous singer
Along Delaware Avenue…

I look out, and now on
The shed edge, a cat,
Arched back like
A skeptical eyebrow.
Chimney smoke rolls through
The black sky above six narrow
Backyards like cemetery plots
In the dead of winter.
And Art Tatum
Plays
"Gone with the Wind."

CARGO CULT

You could spin the dial all
Night – Spin? Dial? What am I
Saying? – and find nary a song
To stir a soul, unless
Static parts on a slice of
Jungle alley between corporate
Towers, some tin-roof cinder
Block universe off Bora Bora
And Zanzibar. The jock wears shorts,
And flip flops that flap
Like cocodrillo jaws as he climbs
After coconuts then spins
78s left by a one-eyed
Jug-eared drifter in the 1940s:
Jack Frum he come back.
The acetate discs in sleeves
Crumbling like mummies' linen,
Mummies that were the subjects
Of love songs on lyres.
The records all the better for
The scratches, like tears
In silk and lovingly cradled
In a stickered grip. Slum
Street harmonizing and rooftop
Ballroom crooning, hearts breaking
At tent show Saturday nights.

78s seated each like a Latin
Dark goddess on leatherette,
Painting her lips in the rear
View mirror of her boy's Havana
1947 Fleetline. A skeleton
Skull in the dashboard
Where the radio used to be.

WALKING WITH AMY BETH

East of the art gallery where
Animal faces wished
To stay hidden, and swaying
Scythes marked time 'til
The end of the vernissage.

And so we passed
The Great Wall on the window
Of the Chinese bar and saw two
Cloth slippers on a lawn, left
Maybe by some supplicant
From the east on Dundas West,
And twenty suns there were
In a sunflower circle.

A shiny-eyed beggar
Out front of the beer store, clean
Clothes and fifty-odd years, "I'm
Not a bum, I'm a party
Animal. You have forty cents?"

Past cigarette lighter towers
Like a Corbu Vladivostok Hell
Where half-boasting, half-
Ashamed R. told of sexing
Morning, noon and night three
Guys, no names, one day. What
Future brags and regrets now
Transpire behind cataract windows?

So we make our rounds, same
As friends from settler days
Or Hittite times to sparrow
And starling accompaniment
And bird-like chatter of the tiny
Rumanian with transfers in
His rolled umbrella.
Abutments of railroad
Overhead and in the roadway
Verge, raccoon eyes are as bright
As a beerstore beggar's.

Gallery display had nothing
On this: God's own Saturday
Installation, but part of it,
And we too.

GOING NOWHERE

My face in subway window, two A.M.
Toronto Sunday morning all
Plains and angles, pea eyes
Peer from walnut shells
Like giving up the three-
Card Monte game.
Cheek seams rivers through
Nahanni cliffs.

My face on subway going
Home from downtown job,
1964, Friday evening
In Philadelphia, angle-
Free and smooth, wild night
Ahead and everything to sketch
Upon window's empty tablet.

I sketched there just one year
Later one dead wife. Drew scenes
In a hundred rooming houses,
And near as many countries left
Marks of my passing. Friends gone
But not erased. Some lovers
Now smudges, some scars,
Some healed over. Jail cells
Made vertical bars on upper
Lip. Concrete floors slept
On upon my forehead. See
Ineffable traces of not
Infrequent episodes of self-
Loathing, as well as insomnia's

weary patina. (Neither
Does it help being badmouthed
In print.)

But note, please, a cocky
Twinkle and slight curl
Of lip in defiance. Quite
The mug, really, and still
There, sixty-first year, in two A.M.
Sunday subway window.

AT ELECTION TIME I ALWAYS
THINK OF MY FATHER

In the apartment living room, Settlement
House out the window, in command.
Mogul for days or a week. No longer
Working the street like a sentry
With a cigar to Tony Bennett
Accompaniment, "Must I Forever Be
A Beggar?" Just now no Bumstead
Of the rowhouses, head tucked between
Shoulders during harridan
Harangues but the big
Ward Leader.

To me who spent whole Saturdays
On the high plains or in canyons
Of the Italia, the tabletop
Was like changing matinee locations.
Gotham in the afternoons, Monument
Valley by nightfall.
Like the little girl with the rag doll
Hiding behind the woodpile
From marauding redskins,
My mother huddled in the bedroom
As riff raff climbed the stairs,
Ward heelers come to get
The gelt, wampum to make
Things right and assure the inevitable
Victory. Hail the Machine.

Me watching from the sofa
Between four goombahs, all
Eyes on the money but noses pointed
Each in a different direction.

Then comes the tall black man
Like a prince with attendant and
Vined down in broadcloth and wool
Worsted. The white men like shabby
Poilu that time in the Marseilles
Station when the Legion
In full dress with dazzling
Kepis marched through. He
Wore slim brown and white
Kicks, and creases might draw blood
From Republicans. My father
And the black man speaking
In code indecipherable except
For daddy-o's "Not unless you
Got no choice."

The summit done, I dogged
Their polished heels down
Spavined stairs. And at the curb,
He spoke to the bodyguard
Who flipped me a silver dollar. I
Watched it turning somersaults
In the city air against red brick
And dishwater sky and caught
It without looking, one-
Handed which made
The black prince grin
Just like great
Jack Johnson.

And they vanished in the dreamboat
Cream tan-top Cadillac. Then
The others hit the bricks, scurrying
To social clubs and corner
Luncheonettes, to hand out new
Dollars to widows of men slain
Over Kemoy or Matsu, and mothers
With polio kids who clattered
When they walked, like pick-up sticks.

And back up tenement stairs,
The table already stashed
In the closet like a nasty
Secret. My father slumped
Before the TV set, and was made
To rise again for a bathroom
Towel to protect the cozy
Morris chair from the oil
Of his hair, so un-
Happy there, the big
Ward Leader.

ROLLERBOARD BLUES

Everything's dead below the waist,
His face rearranged by shrapnel,
A Ranch Hand lain upon his back. Still,
He seems a good-natured sort, smiling
Thui rolling through District One
On his stomach, pads on elbows, guitar
On folded-back rag doll legs. Making
His rounds because some joker
Gave him a guitar and he learned
A couple of chords in the Western
Scale. And Thui, phonetically,
Sings "Don't Be Cruel."
Then another joker – it wasn't me –
Taught him some old blues. And now you
See him calling at sidewalk cafés
Of happy Westerners with backpacks. Big
Girls before big meals, guys behind
Camcorders, all drinking Tigers or Bah
Bah Bahs. Thui sets them up
With "Don't Be Cruel" and at the precise
Moment when they're smiling
Into that shattered face, hits them
With that old John Lee Hooker, about
How you're so beautiful but
You're gonna die some day.
And then he rolls away, smiling.

DEMOCRATIC VISTAS

Walt, I see before me now that place
Where they laid you down: Harleigh,
And the dark grey mausoleum, graffiti-ed,
Ringed round by iron-spoked fence, razor-
Wire topped. Across the street, a hospital
Where Puerto Rican taxi driver hollers
By the emergency door at black welfare
Woman fare. Beyond, a street such as any
Other in your Camden, broken glass,
And gutted cars dead on their rims,
Deserted in the sunshine of a summer
Afternoon, save for six-and-a-half
Foot young shadows fleeing around
A corner. How can it be that the ground
Itself does not sicken, O great
Grey poet? Rise up and walk your America.
Walt Whitman, you were one of the roughs,
A kosmos.
Under a late moon half-risen slip
Between the plywood sheets
Of a row house doorway – the door unscrewed
From jamb for winter fires – and steal up
The stairs. Lie down between bride
And groom on the piss-stained
Mattress, cuddle both in deep
Crack sleep and rise to behold daybreak
At the glass-less window. Does anything
Sweet grow out of such corruptions?
Does refinery air taste good
To your palate? Ah! What chemistry!
Do you see spread out

Your prophesized democratic vistas,
Or scream a barbaric lament
Over the roofs of these States?

ROCKET 88

Vroom! Vroom!
Top up the tank with forty litres
Of gold illusions, and pretend
You're leaving it behind.
Often it's the only way
For even a highway-weary fool. Leave,
Leave it bitter in the breakfast nook
Or faking it in bed. Leave it like a lawn half-
Mown or a letter you can't bear to mail.
Leave it at the office. Let the doctor deal
With it. Leave it frowning, arms akimbo
On the porch where the light
Is never on anyway. At least, not
For the likes of you. Spray gravel
On petunias and opinions of you
As you begin what's become nearly
An annual trek. Ram it in gear,
Pilgrim. Put the pedal
To the metal, and get thee gone.

It's been working for me since
About 1961. I've cut out in Cadillacs,
Chevies and Fords, and, Christ,
Chryslers I'd nearly forgotten.
Have convinced myself I'm a Roadmaster
Of Valiant journeys. Gone in Desotos,
Studebakers and Olds, all of which
No longer exist, same as my reasons. They
Don't make them like they used to. For now
I can see that which I flee. One hand
Aching around the Hurst handle, the other

Numb on the suicide knob. I can beat
On the dashboard and bypass the muffler
But not still the rumble of promises
From the running board days.
In the rear view, Buerger's looming
Large. In the side view, objects
Are more dangerous than they appear.
Vroom! Vroom!
One never knows what's lurking behind
The billboard or treading foul water
In ditches. What road-kill will rise up
And declare itself. It cruises the freeways
And sees everything. Watches from the eyes
Of the backdeck doggy.
The last roadblock's somewhere
Over the shimmering horizon. I know,
I know I'm not firing on all cylinders,
Guzzling too much of the leaden past.
Pig iron for the junkyard and the crusher
But grant me a few more kilometres
And I'll give you a run for your money,
Taunt you with my glass pacs, lay
Rubber on your inevitable intentions.
I'll drive all night through the plague
Lands and stop on Boot Hill, shoot
Dice on a fresh dug grave
Then over the top and – Vroom!
Vroom! — Gone.

CREEKERS

A winter day like most others, except
It comes slant-wise, the rain, like
Movie rain, and gives a spasm
Of hope. But, no; no sunshine
At my window's perimeter. Nor
Are these hard tropical bullets
Of monsoon. Even the cedar trees
Are fed up, their shoulders slumped
Like a green hobo army in sodden
Greatcoats, trooping back to Elphinstone.
The Sunshine Coast! – some developer's
Real estate scam; he'd already named
Greenland. But the Weekly announces
Activity aplenty. Crop circle lectures
And wiccan retreats. Let's sit by the ocean
And talk of Baba Ram Dass. Tonight
At the Hall, "Real Funky Blues," it says
"Come Dance the Night Away." Thanks
But I'll stay here with my own
Music and wine.
The audience would only be vegans
And astrologers and balding men my age
With ponytails, patrolling
For booze breath, who've
Spent the day showing
Each other their crystals.
They'll kick off their sandals
And gum boots and Get Down
In wool socks, waving scarves
(I'm embarrassed thinking about it)
Tomorrow, in front of each other's

Homes, they'll march for peace,
Sign petitions, email the proper
Authorities but take no chances.
They never have, and they
Never will. As sure
As the rain will fall.

MOTOROLA WRANGLERS

Campfire stones like cement stoops.
A palomino Cadillac with white fetlocks
Snorting in the tall asphalt
And young desperadoes
Warming chapped hands at the fire hydrant.
From their aeries, swooping birds:
Flamingoes, Robins, Ravens,
And Sonny Till and the Orioles, all
Calling strange harmonies
In brick canyons, before the morning
Of reform school, of the factory,
The office, the Moyamensing –
There under limitless skies
In the Motorola plastic
Portable radio night.

SAIGON JOE

Bug-eyed, foul breathed, muttering
Saigon Joe in the middle of mosaiced
Sidewalks of old Catinet Street. He's
Like a buoy in the river just
Over there, marking channels, two
Strands that will never meet.
Pedestrians swing around his
Imploring.

His mother, from Le Quong, knew
2,700 G.I.s and others before
She could get out and she never
Came once. The tin boat sank
A mile from the sugar refinery
So you could say she never left.

Daddy looked like an old-time field
Hand, cotton picker like Alan Lomax
Interviewed, him about to do a jig.
Grew up in a shotgun shack
South of Beaufort, hard by the sea
And was stoned his whole tour.
Went home, let off steam
And shook a jolt
Before getting with the County
Pushing a broom, pulling
A rake, and now 'Nam is only
A three-in-the-morning thing.
Meanwhile his little nappy-headed
Boy does the route: the Grand,
The Rex, The Majestic, shunned
On every sidewalk. Ignored

By Triple-Cut, even, who hops
On his only appendage and flaps
Suppurating stumps like an ostrich
With clipped wings in a landmine
Nightmare.

The lottery lady lights
The amputee's cigarette
But no one strikes a match
For Saigon Joe who hears
"In-A-Gadda-Da-Vida"
And Stevie Wonder when
He bends to snatch Heroes
From the gutter, and rises
Bug-eyed, foul breathed,
Muttering.

COME BACK, PRETTY MOMMA

There was a callow youth and
He loved an older woman, age
Of twenty-six. On her thigh
Was a beauty mark just like
The Lonestar State turned
Upside down. I lingered there
At Brownsville where we
Lay on a beach called Baghdad
And played, and played our
Fingers in the sand, squeezing
Handfuls of the future. The Beach
Boys were on the pink transistor
And I pretended I liked them, too.
A meteor fell out of the sky
And landed in a blind man's
Pocket. Men fell through the sky
On the other side of the world,
Having been pushed
By foreigners from
Helicopters. You didn't outlive
That war, having ceased to exist
At the age of thirty-two. And today I'm
On another shore, once more
With the Beach Boys. They're
Right over there, the ones
Who are left, under palms. I
Listen because you liked them.
And I squeeze tight handfuls
Of the past.

Nassau, 14 January 2007

DREAM OF DINNERTIME, 1958

Ma and Pa like Claire and Francis
Hand in hand levitating above
The table, their dreams like the hurled –
Not five minutes ago – serving dish
Shattered against the wall with orchids,
And now coming back together as
In a film in reverse. Her
Screeching turned to a coloratura's
Sweet cavatinas; his grunts basso
Profundo harmonies to Mills
Brothers' melodies in his mind.
Tonight the ceiling cracks reveal
The star-light slivers usually hidden
At suppertime. There are truffles
In tubs and terrines, caviar
Boats and lobster on a silver platter on
A table that never was embarrassed by
Frozen Salisbury Swanson steaks or string
Beans boiled to mush. That cow gliding
Through shotgun rooms waves a hoof
At my father seated on the chandelier
Like it was a curbside in heaven,
And two musical rabbis, Sam and Izzy
From Grossman's Kosher, ride
The dining room jet stream; they're
Not dirty Jews tonight.
And there's my mother Isadora-ing
In gauzy gown and bombazine.
And they, Ma and Pa, tear
Their eyes away one from
The other to beam upon

Their son who surely has no need
To run away from home
And never will.

GIBRALTAR POINT

Like an oil drilling rig
Doing calisthenics on
The beach, then photographing
Childish sculptures
At the water's edge. Real ducks,
Him and her, eye driftwood
Version. When tentative quacks
Get no response they
Waddle away, to the other side of the
Picnic log – there was a fire in its
Belly, their love nest – Me, I'm
Solitary, no mate, sixty-two
Next month. Am I going
Crazy by the water as the lake
Tide slips in and out doing it's
Sit-ups on the shore or is this
Really living?

CONSORTING WITH THE ENEMY

1

Pumping gas in Virginia, summer
Of 1963 outside the gates
Of Fort Lee, the nervous corporal
Just returned from a place where
The U.S. military wasn't, called
Vietnam, told of helicopter
Interrogations, pushing Cong
Out the door and watching their
Cartoon caterwauling. "I laughed
Then," he said. "I can't sleep now."

2

At the Highlands long house
In a tribal town, the skeletons
Of elephants bombed by B52s
Because every elephant like
Every bicycle was a potential
Enemy, hauling for those very
Same Cong.

3

At the lunch stop, bus route, Hanoi-
Da Nang. Walking back, the soldier
Son of a soldier my age, one of those
Gook guerrillas, takes my hand
As men do here, and women too, to
Stress his point and in friendship.

4

In Hanoi hotel room, the jazz
Club girl with thin limbs
And round face and same sounds
As women everywhere, no razor
Blades down there like
The flattop sergeant said
That long ago morning when I
Didn't take the big step forward
From which there would be
No returning.
And here I am now,
Consorting.

LOLLYGAGGING MOON

Balloon floats with brown
Leather-like feet on the zocalo.
Inflatable television characters
With ancient people
On a string.

Then in a puff of wind one woman
Rises from the cobblestones and
Soon is looking down on tingas
And chimichangas, Franny's bench
And Germans. High above hotel lobby
Folk dancing and out past city limits
Across Indian land toward a sky
Darker than mole sauce.

I can see Orion's Belt on Bob's
Sponge pants and a cat's paw
Cloud just missed good old Daffy
Duck to lie across
A lollygagging moon.

And the woman cuts her strings
To float free in the Azteca,
Zacateca, Iroquois, Chippewa,
Yaruma, Tarahumara
Taino, Arapahoe
Heavens
To see if
The moon's a balloon
And the Great Spirit but
A puff
Of wind.

ECSTASY AND ME

I saw you showing off
At that party. You made
A teeter-totter of the room.
All the men over on your side
Women on the other, up
In the air and me with them.
You worked it, too, never
Allowing how it was me who
Took the mop out of your hands
And wrote you a woman of un-
Fathomable depths, painted
You that smile of enchantment,
Put oceans of time
In your eyes, gave you
The gilded mirror to hold up
And it's their own longing
Looking back. And what do you see,
Staring at the plastic
Other side? Anything besides
A way to pay the rent and make
A buck on the side? Ah,
No sense being bitter. I made
Your bed and my own, and have
To sleep in the latter, no
Matter where it may be. And
I finally tore the craving
Out of my heart and put it
In theirs. I made you mystery
And can unmake you, too. I need
But say the words and you'll
Have worry lines and smoker's
Breath and sagging breasts. Me,

All I need to do is hit the road
With a little close-up work and
Some new long-range dreaming.
Make a pass with my magic broom
And sweep you under the rug.
See some other Hungarian
Face on the walls of budget
Rooms. Conjure me another
Hedy Lamarr from a house-
Wife.

TORONTO STORY

"I'm going to kill you, yo!" shouted Belmiro Britto,
fourteen, of Margueretta Street.
"Yo, don't kill me, mutha fucker, yo!" replied Duarte
"The Rabbit" Coelho, fourteen, from near Bloor and
    Concord.
They heard each other, but since they wore or
Were born with headphones in place, heard not
The Pop Pop Pop Pop! when Doneel
Rashid Green, sixteen, from Jane and the 401,
Tugged the trigger of his little
Mouse gun – a semi, 32. calibre and cute
As a button with the three-inch barrel, bullets
No bigger than kidney stones, putting one in the neck
And one in the heart – the other two going wildly
Astray like a couple of Jack Russell terriers just
Let off the leash, and shattering the glass of the soft
Drink door – of Duk-Ho Pak, thirty-four. It couldn't
    immediately
Be determined from whence he hailed because his
Wife who spoke no English was hysterical,
Getting the news via police pantomime, down
At the corner variety store. This being where
She put in twelve hours a day with only a cat
In Halloween colours for company, cat that slept
On top of the lottery ticket machine, lifting
One ear whenever it heard that machine go:
"Gagnon! Gagnon!"

Doneel Rashid Green, sixteen, only had one bad
Moment before he shot Duk-Ho Pak, but rapped
To himself:

I'm a stone bad mutha fucka
And I mustn't weaken
What would my baby girl
Then be thinkin'?
For me there'd be no more freakin
So I put three in that L'il Korean

And only lost his gangsta cold-chisel
Stare for the split-second the blood went
SPURT SPURT SPURT out
Of the neck of Duk-Ho Pak, regaining it, his
Cool, quick as he'd lost it, thinking how he'd
Tell it to his crew out front of the complex
By the stone fountain, dried-up he liked to say,
Like his thirty-one year old momma's future,
SPURTING, he'd tell them, like when you've
Been pulling your meat.

Doneel Rashid Green, sixteen, in baggy black
Denim, looking almost like a little boy
In his daddy's jeans with a water
Pistol in his hand, stepped out
Onto January's ice grey sidewalks under
A dirty dishwater sky, got his shoulders
Dipping and rising in rhythm, put some heel
And toe into it, feeling good on those air
Soles with gang colour laces, bought, like
The mouse gun, off the Net. Feeling like he
Might just float on up to desperado Heaven
For a quick look-see and what's happening
With Tupac, let him know there's another
Pistolero in town; yeah, felt good for half
A block until Travis Leech, twenty-nine, born here,
And Alixi Gruvinov, thirty-three, from Kazakhistan,
Originally – he with the stiff blond

Hair combed back that looked like troughs
In waves of a muddy sea. Alixi
Gruvinov was on the force a year
And a half before he realized why they
Called him "Comb Grooves" – Travis
Had a crewcut –
In Indigo uniforms, they stepped
From behind the parking lot wall
On the far side of the pizza place and hollered,
"Police! Halt!" But Doneel Rashid Green, sixteen,
Wasn't down for any of that shit, and raised
Sideways the cute little mouse gun. Alixi
Crying "No!" and hollering into his shoulder:
"Incident. Incident. Back up!" and Doneel got
Off four more – POP POP POP POP – that missed
The cops entirely but took out the windows
Of the pizza place, chunks of glass falling
Like humungous dominoes, then Alixi's .38 said
BOOM BOOM BOOM and put the kid down with
Three grouped tight in the chest (going
For mass, like they'd said at the Academy)
And Doneel Rashid Green, sixteen, took to the air, not
To pay his call on Tupac but to twirl up there
Just above the ice-grey sidewalk like strange
Dark pizza dough; finally hitting cold
Concrete, where his young body emptied
Itself of his young life's blood – SPURT
SPURT SPURT SPURT. Meanwhile,
A young woman walked out of the Bikrami
Method Yoga Studio across the street, looking
Like she was talking to herself, glanced over
And immediately away and continued social
Networking. And Alixi Gruvinov was bent over,
Hands on knees, breathing, breathing hard, like
He'd just broken his personal best

In the marathon at the Police Games, and Travis
Leech offered manly pats on the back. And the blood
That had been in Doneel Rashid Green, sixteen, spread
Like an ink blot and the blood that had been
In Duk-Ho Pak, forty-four, seeped under the door
Of the internet café and down slippery steps
As if to make its getaway, rushing
To mingle with that of Doneel Rashid Green,
Sixteen, and...
"I'm going to kill you, yo," shouted Belmiro
Britto, fourteen, of Margueretta Street, and
Duarte "the Rabbit" Coelho, fourteen, from Concord
And Bloor called back, "No, don't kill me,
Muthafucker, yo!"

DREAMING OF ADOLPH

His right arm rises
As the sun collapses way out west
On Bloor Street. He salutes the end
Of day with an aerosol can in his hand.
Hails the Korean Star Café
And, without invading, chicken dances
In front of the Poland, wanders
Across town muttering jabberwocky
German, even nods
To the JCC, which he might deface
But the ball only rattles at the end
Of his arm, hisses as he declaims
With spittle sporadic as an erratic
Lawn sprinkler in these concrete canyons.
Toothbrush moustache grown over
Yellow dentures, shoe polish black back
Hair combed forward on balding crown.
A little tramp, his jackboots
Duct-tapped sneakers, swatches
For swastikas. Adolph
Who'd for decades hunkered
In bunkers, granted refugee
Status but banned from beer halls.
Poor lost vegan, dreadnaught
Pockets filled with carrots and bad
Drawings, shuffling through puddles,
Old pinball machine eyes frantic
For Goering and Goebbels, loiters
Near Queen's Park buildings flinging
Lighted books of matches, telling
Constables communists did it.

Some quaint maniac of the old
Breed superseded by slick mis-
Directors, media electronic conglomerates
Whose deeds succeed where bygone
Demigods could only dream.

A COMPETENT MAN

"He's handsome," you said, in
A classic sort of way, and still
Vigorous, jogs every other day,
Makes a good living and built
Your studio all by himself. Like
A gunfighter with his tool belt,
Orange pencil behind his ear.
One sees him around town
In a grey Land
Rover, winch caked with skookum
Mud. All this you told me as
We lay there, your head in the nest
Between my shoulder and chest,
Afterwards.

DEAR MARY

It's me again your faithful
Correspondent. Maybe you noticed
There's no censor's stamp on this one.
It's a long story but no,
I didn't finally make parole.

I saw you with another man today.
Yes, I did. He looks like
He has plenty of what it takes
To get along in the world.
Maybe he'll love little Jessie
As if she were his own but she's
Not. She's mine and yours.

There was something about the way
You looked at him. Something
To your posture that wasn't right.
Bet he has an ex-wife or two. Owns
A house, a boat, buys you
A diamond ring for Christmas,
Baby. But he'll never
Take you to Cambodia.

I got a woman, too. It's
Really true, and she
Loves me as much as you
Used to say you do.

Well, okay, I made that up.
Both parts of it. I will have
A woman soon, one who

Loves me like that. Just wait,
You'll see; she and I
On the same street as him and you.
We might nod to each other.
Maybe it'll get to the point where
We even say "hello." And after
You've gone a few steps
The guy with plenty of what it takes
To get along in the world will
Ask you who that was and you'll
Tell him: "Oh, it's just some guy I
Used to know back in another
Time and another place and far
Away on the other side of town,
And the other side of plenty
Of other towns."

Then he'll take your tender little hand
In both his great big paws, and look
In your eyes, tell you he hopes
You'll love him, too, someday.
Which reminds me, that line
In one of the only two letters
You ever wrote to me? The bit
About how you love me like
A laundress loves her linens? Well
We have a library in the joint
So imagine how I felt when I
Figured out you stole that line.

Anyway, I want to be loved
Before work and after hours,
Too. Yeah,
Maybe someday.

In the meantime, I'm sending you
These things I found at the bottom
Of a steamer trunk, that one
I stored at the hideout with
Little Larry. Just a few photographs –
Note the one of the two sleepy
People too much in love, one of them
Thought, to ever say good night...
And here's a bottle of moisturizer, a
Burnt spoon, a couple of syringes.
And these skimpy undergarments.
I certainly don't want them around.

Do you still have religion? Me,
I'm trying to be like St. Francis,
And a little bird told me you'd
Joined the Chamber of Commerce
And that your monthly talks inspire
The hell out of all of them. I can
Well believe it, remembering some
Of the things you inspired me to do. I hear
You tell them how anyone can
Overcome anything, then offer
Personal anecdotes about surviving
A disastrous relationship. Is
That what we had? A "relationship"?
Well at least it means you were
Thinking of me. Do you tell them
You were known as the Jones Girl,
Mention the lush rolling and joint-
Copping back of the Carnegie?
How about the snitch and dope fiend
You ran off to Mexico with? Or is he
Part of the Chamber of Commerce, too?

And that same bird said you've
Taken up golf. Who could ever
Have imagined? Not me.
You in those funny clothes one
Has to wear? And the shoes
With the spikes on the bottom. Of
Course, you probably like them.

Look, Mary, the thing is, I'm
On the lam. Went over the wall
At dawn, knocked a bull over the head,
Stole the laundry truck and sneaked
Into town just for a glimpse of you.
And I got it this afternoon, you with
The guy who looks like he has plenty
Of what it takes to get along in the world.

Well, that's it. I can hear the hound dogs
Baying in the alley. I'm going out
The trap door, heading south.

See you on the links.
                    John

IN THE DESERT

She wore a silk robe, the colour
Of crème de menthe. In back
Of her, a mountain, up which
Right now, loggers are moving
With their machinery. And her
Eyes were tunnels. Looking
Into them, he felt he was standing
On a high ledge and about to lose
All balance. Later, he will wonder
If he made silly windmill gestures
With his arms, as if struggling
To maintain his place in the middle
Of the dirt road, in the world.
Or maybe it was merely the meds,
What they gave him when he got
Back from that war in that place
Where the ruins of Mareb,
At Sheba, stuck out of the sand
Like shattered bones.
Those were not Roman Legions
They vaporized but fellaheens raised
To Allah. And he came back with
A radio station's hubbub in his head.
A torturer for a top jock, and the all-night
Show screaming all day. And her there
In the robe of silk, eyes like holes
In the night. Balkis, Queen of Sheba.
Ostrich feathers and ebony bracelets,
And her bodyguard of dwarfs.

She stepped down from a piebald
Horse and they went walkabout –
She with a fetching limp,
Speaking in riddles – through
This vanishing civilization.

THE GAP

I woke on a cantina floor
In the Darien Gap.
The night before was a big
Hole in my memory. But I had
An itch that I'd never had before.
Outside was mostly mud and midgets,
And one of the latter was being
Serviced by another just like him
Who was on his knees in the former.
Rain ran from all the tin roofs
Of town, sheets of it like
Pages of a biography that was
Beginning to bore its protagonist.
So I did what I'd done in the other
Chapters: I had a drink and then
Another one, and the woman who
Invited me back to her crib was
An amputee, reminiscent
Of the dead-legged lady in the African
Chapter and not all that unlike the neurotic
Vancouver ecologist in some
Other part of the tome.
Soon I fled that place, too. The jungle
Resembled the backs of parading
Irishmen; there were a million snakes
Dangling like angry neckties. I walked
Across a stream on the backs
Of crocodiles, encountered the requisite
French Foreign Legionnaire loner,
All alone in the crotch of a Ceiba tree
His head and neck twisted

Like a question mark,
And peccaries were eating his feet.

Well, to be succinct, I walked the Gap,
And bridged the hemispheres. Completed
Yet another chapter and volume, only
To get a bad review from the usual
Torontonian. I've seen him
Sitting bland-faced on Bloor Street,
With his laptop on the patio. "I don't
Believe most of it, anyway," he sniffed
In print. But he wished he could
Have taken the place
Of either of the midgets.

CALLOW MARINER

No Captain Korzeniowski or gaviero
Maqroll, looking from cabin or crow's nest.
Mere deckhand, Cape May, New Jersey-
Lewes, Delaware ferry; later worked
Passage San Fran-Honolulu and back.
No saloon-wrecking tough sailors'
Brawls nor Chief Stewards trying
To bugger me. There were a couple
Of tavern scuffles, four ports, not
As many girls; some decent yarns.
At every side were shorelines
Where cranes looked like bending palms,
And vice versa, or asphalt fields
Of automobiles. At night,
I rarely raised my head
To the famous mariners' night
Where heaven and sea turned
Topsy-turvy. For I was old enough
To feel absurd for looking, yet
Young enough to peek at all that
Space and time and place for some sign,
Some image of her, gone already
In her youth and mine.
So mostly I stole time
From ordinary chores for staring
Over rails, contemplating seas
Layered like Macedonia. Green-
Blue-grey gradations with red
Snapper, tuna, dorado, flying fish
Sea lice, electric eels, turtles
Like buoys and older than Ahab; truck

Tires; a cage big enough for a lion
Or three slaves; amphoras, a crate
Of brandy, winches, stocks, a printing
Press, gold pans from 1849; skeletons
Of mail order brides; a leg bone cuffed
To a generator and waving like a flag
That never got planted
In any new world.

FINAL DRIVER

It wasn't merely for a thrill
I stood beside a thousand roads
Hoping for a lift to Venezia
Or Venice Beach. A ride from the good blonde
Wearing a push-up bra in a rag top Packard,
A dashing Chilean who'd known Neruda personally;
Ride from a big butter-and-egg man
Name of Smilin' Jack, had a picnic basket
Of Suffolk ham sandwiches and Falstaffs
In the cooler. "Hep, yo'self, boy," he said.
The ride like Roy Earle got all the way
To L. A. in "High Sierra" with that cozy family
Had a clubfoot girl yearning to love
A guy like me, after the operation.
I would have taken all of those, of course,
Stowing my grip in the backseat, happy
In the time of my life but I was trying
To thumb down the woman with the how,
The guy with the why. Those who'd explain
It all. Why death owned the roadhouses
And why the time of my life was speeding
Past, faster than cacti headed the other way.
The one behind the wheel who'd tell about
The stars and how they got that way.
The why of burrowing owls and dung beetles.

But that's a ride I never got and I expect
You never did, either. It's as if
We're all back where we started,
Stranded in Wawa, waiting
On that final driver.

FOR ME AND MY GAL

There was a harvest moon.
You lay under it on sheets
Faded the colour of leaves that
Fluttered to rest last week.
I had intended to write something else,
About heading west one year,
Working on a ranch in the Boundary
Region. But I noticed it's
A halloween pencil in my hand,
Tossed by a trick or treater, and made
In Taiwan. On it a bat's trapped
In another orange moon, like aspic.
There's a spider been strangled by its web,
And a kohl-eyed ghost grimaces
With his big bag of tricks. Everyone looks
Like they're glad to be dead.
And the expression on the pumpkin
Is that of a lady gave a poisoned
Cocktail to her hubby right before
He killed her with an axe.
Only the leggy witch is lovely, hieing
Cross the wide old sky back
To Medicine Hat, black
Coattails tickling my face
Like dead leaves confetti.

SOMETHING HAPPENING

It was all different when
I walked outside. The trees came
From a model train set. The neighbour
Backing his car was Johnny Stompanato.
Against an Aqua Velva sky came
Tough city sparrows whose pant
Legs were too short. Immense
As cargo planes, they grew but
The usual wires stayed taut. They all
Looked like Two-Ton Tony Galento,
Stared unblinking and flapped their wings.
Clare of St. Francis was spaniel-eyed
On the other side of the picket fence.

Everything was different. But
On their walks to school, the others
Hadn't noticed a thing.
Some flipped cards while the teacher
Sang "Getting to Know You," and I stared
Out the window. Fog
Kept to the corners like burglars
Who'd been too late getting away.
There, where the taproom used to be,
Was a Mosque with ogee arches
And cowboy snipers in the minarets.
Something
Was about to happen sure.

HEY, RUBE!

The carnival tore down
While townies slept the sleep
Of the Just, and woke
To an empty vacant lot.
Only ruts in the mud
A reminder of another world:
An orange bordered, topsy
Turvy world
Of tawdry wonders.

Now the elephant is gone.
It was so friendly and really seemed
To like your daughter. But
It's a good thing you didn't
Let her get too close.
There's a trick the beast
Likes to play with its chain,
Hiding links of it in the sawdust
To lure you closer. That's how
That mean drunk in Tabor
Went to meet his Maker.

The talker in the boater
And the checkered suit, ran
The mitt camp, and was more
Eloquent than any chapter of Joyce?
Weren't you mesmerized
By his dancing moustache, as he
Talked you out of a summer's wages.

You wound up with empty pockets
Watching his taillights blinking their
Message: So long, sucker!

Live two-headed girl!

    She might have been alive once
    For a minute or two back
    In the womb.

Man Eating Fish!
    Sucker, you've been had.

Knock over the bottles, buster.
Win your girl some plush and leave
Her nibbling cotton candy and staring
At Jo Jo, the Dog-Face Boy
While you sneak off for a peek
At the pretty half-and-half.
Pay a dollar extra to touch it, go
Ahead nobody has to know.

Some of the fellows went to the kooch show
Didn't see enough of what they expected
To see or a guy got testy cause he developed
Strange feelings for Harriet the Hirsute Girl. He's
A proper citizen and this can't be happening,
Must have slipped something in his beer, those
Carnies, so he lashes out at the pinhead
And the torso man, at Commodore Nutt and Billy,
The boy with a tail. And his buddies
In ball caps join him, hollering
About freaks and geeks. That's
When a roughie

Or a rideboy or Harry the Button
Made with a "Hey, Rube!" on the loud
Hailer and the whole lot went crazy,
Light bulbs popping, noses busting, prancing
Ponies torn loose from the carousel, some
Guy firing a thirty-thirty from the top
Of the Ferris wheel and Cannonball
Kazinski arcing over the lot like
A misbegotten missile, as Saint Vitus
Rolls his bones and dances across
The tops of the tents
Of the Devil's Midway.

The Push sprung the boys
From jail, and canvas collapsed
As good citizens slept the sleep
Of the Just, and the caravan pulled
Out into the dawn taking a couple
Of townies along for the ride, one
Being the DA's comely young daughter,
The other that strange child
The mayor and his wife kept
Hidden in the basement.

By October and the final tear down
The Mayor's daughter was pregnant
By the alligator boy. And won't it be
Something next year when the Ten-
In-One returns and she shows off
Proud hubby and the newborn
To the family she left back home.

LOVE GREETINGS IN THE MARKET PLACE

Assembled 4 May 2004, from written material placed in Auckland
hotel room: "Auckland A-Z," "City Scene" and the Holy Bible:
Mark: Chapter 12.

In the Bay of Sunshine, he built a tower
And he leased it. Dug a place
For the wine vat. Whose image is this,
Really? Clinton made a very public
Call: You shall love your neighbours
Like Angels of Heaven. And was tapped
Once all over at the High Art Glass
Gallery. But those vine dressers said:
Don't plant Miss Rawka,
And Jesus answered: "Now that
You are here, have you not even read
This scripture: 'Swing by sometime,
Oedipus Rex?'" Blue water
Dreams and tiles. Pharisees
And Herodians will take possession
Sometime in the Resurrection
On Upper Khartoum Place. All
Dog owners cock an ear: "Beware
Of the scribes, who desire to go around
In long robes. These will receive
Greater condemnation."

SKAGWAY

"Reason I've been looking at you," she
Said, bending over the table, lining
Up her shot, "is because you remind me
Of a fella I was in love with once."

Weighty breasts swayed over green baize
Like twin hammocks over a close-cropped lawn.
She sank the eight ball with a crisp shot
And raised eyebrows in my direction, as if
The winning play was fraught
With what was sure to come. She
Collected her winnings from a guy
With a corduroy face, and sprang
For a round of drinks. At the bourbon-coloured
Bar she nudged me with her hip. I
Looked out above the swinging doors.
It was still Skagway in November
And icy rain still coming down.
There were board sidewalks and bored
Old men. A cruise ship way out in the grey
But none of them were about to come in here.

"That guy you remind me of, he was better
Looking than you." She waited, and I told her,
"Well, plenty of them are." "But he wasn't
All that hot in bed."
"That's too bad," I said. Her flannel shirt
Was tucked into tight jeans. She hooked thumbs
In the waistband on either side
Of a Mack truck buckle and rolled her hips,
Rolled them around and around. "He didn't

Have no hip action. You have any
Hip action?"
"I guess it depends on who you ask."

She whispered in my ear and I nodded
And we made our way past the pool table,
Down the dim hall between washrooms
And telephones and out the back door.
A sheet of rain slid off the overhang
Like one long roll of typewriter paper.
"Right here!" she said and undid the buckle,
Shook down her jeans like a wet dog, big
Pink panties following the jeans, and stepped
One leg out of them like a sourdough majorette
Breathing hard. She bent over a trashcan,
Her legs spread wide because she was so tall
It was a great big rounded Reubens' ass
And we made cans and lids rattle and clatter
To the ground. She moaned and cursed
And announced what was going to happen. There
Was a loud tintinnabulation when it did and
She gasped how good it had been: "You're
A great fuck!" she said, and I said, "Thank you."
We pulled up our pants and went back
Into the bar. "That deserves another drink,"
She said and bought us two, and then four.
The big woman asked me to come home with her
And said I could stay for however long I wished,
Maybe get on with the YWPR, make a life of it
With her. When I said No to all of it, for I was
Dawson City-bound, she threw
Her glass on the floor, ice cubes skittering
Like dice. "You bastard! Think you can treat
Me like that. Get away from me."

I finished my drink and got away from her, kept
Walking to the exit. "And you're a lousy fuck!"
She hollered. "Worst fuck I ever had! You don't
Have a clue what to do!"

They all watched as I went on my way, out
The swinging doors, some wondering if it were
True, and all glad it wasn't them. I heard
My boot heels clacking
On the wooden boards,
Keeping time:
Worst... fuck ... I
Ev ... er ... had ... don't ... have a clue
What ... to do ... Worst ... fuck
I ... ev ... er ... had ... don't ... have
A clue
What ... to ... do

WEST END BLUES

Big blonde in a purple slip
Lies sleeping. I turn her head
To face me. The beauty mark
On her nose in the street lamp
Light. I watch as so often I do
On sleepless nights.
I've never told her.
It's the anniversary of the death
Of Louis Armstrong. There are
Russian ships in the Sound, unless
Since dinner they've stolen away.
A man down the hall has lived
In the hotel for forty years.
I got off the plane today from Vietnam.
Where are the other passengers now?
Outside two men giggling. The moon
Is balanced at the very top of a cedar tree.
Passing clouds make it spin, like
A basketball on a fingertip.
I watch you. Your beauty proclaims
Itself in the night.

MY LOCAL

There it was in the clearing
Like a tin and bamboo vulva
Slashed out of the liana
Architecture. Swinging doors
Kept the beat and on the floor
Were the crushed bones
Of those who'd tippled before.
Time stood still in a pile
In the corner, all the watches
That lined the inside of the greatcoats
Of goniffs, and that nobody needed
Anymore. The bartender was Fritz
Who'd had the same job in The
Sorcerer; he looked like he'd been
Pouring them and wiping the walnut
Since Zumarraga ordered his first
Sherry Flip. The bouncer was a cretin
But he never gave anyone
The old heave-ho. Working
Girls crowded round, and
One of them looked like Olive Oil. Mean-
While a goat that chewed tobacco
Was looking in the window. He seemed to be
Plotting something, like Lenin in Zurich.
And above the bar was a photo of Arthur
Cravan. "Fritz," I said, "You wouldn't know it
But I'm a kind of poet and I got..." And he
Said, "Yah, go on and tell it." Even though
He'd probably heard it a thousand times
Before. So I let them have it,
Concentrating on the part about you.

When I was done, Fritz nodded and so
Did I, and the girls nodded, the cretin
Nodded and also the goniffs,
And we all resembled those
Plastic bar birds, pecking at their drinks.
Then Olive Oil took me upstairs
And her stomach looked
Like an aerial view of the jungle
From the top of boot hill, green
Lichen fringes around red swatches
Where the planes dropped chemicals
To clear a path for the highway
That never showed up. Back downstairs
The drinks would always be free, and
On the jukebox they were playing my song.
It was there right between Frankie "Half Pint"
Jaxon and the Boswell Sisters, "I Got a
Girl Just Like a Rock Inside my Shoe."

It had been a long road
But I'd finally made it home.

LEEDS

There you are every time I look
Out the window. Your name at night
Like silver script on the indigo label
Of an old Decca 1978. I laugh
At the thought of a street named
After the likes of you anywhere, save
In a haven of fiends. Naturally, the
Sign is listing and'll probably fall over
Just like you did the first night we met,
At Cody's Bar, from the stage to the floor,
No flailing, you and the bass, and some
Wiseacre hollered, "Timber!"
But you kept on playing. Now front row
Angels come to rub against your pole, and last
Night I seemed to hear the street sign wonder
In a mutter, how high the moon.

PHNOM PENH BLUES

I'm leaning on the balcony and she's
Holding up a lamppost
Down on Sisowath Quay.
There's a guy behind shades
In a Lexus. We're all looking
For something to call our own, another
Kind of key, the one'll unlock
The fabled Silver Palace. She's sixteen
With dark legs in short skirt, a cute
Little rear and her blouse
Is a couple of years old. Fat
White guys over Anchors
Are drawing straws. They flew over
From Saigon. "You can get 'em younger
Over here," one says.
There's a parade of miracles passing,
Jetsam of the Khmer Rouge. You could
Fill a pagoda with their missing limbs.
I try pretending that compared to theirs
My own woes are a robust lot. But
It doesn't help. Kali's over my
Shoulder. Buddha's down the block
And doesn't want any of it. There's
No Veronica to cloak my eyes.
I can shed a Tonle Sap of tears.
They'll flood a delta, grow
A brand new nightmare crop.

PROLOGUE TO A CANTERBURY TALE

I drive south on the left hand
Side, along a wild coast where
The wind bends Nikau palms like
Catapults. The stones are
Shuttlecocks, and erode the faces
Of boney women out front of faded
Caravans. The men all look
Like they've eaten too many meat pies.
At Greymouth people talk to me
And I don't know what they are saying.
This has happened to me elsewhere.
The magnates knew what they were
Doing, starting here, the kind of place
You get out of quick and return only
When it doesn't work out. I
Have a friend who followed in the train
Of the very first brown-skinned, white-
Robed wise man passing through.

Cottages are nearly smothered
In flowers; it's all so quaint but
Are women touching themselves
As the big engine
Roars through the valley?

For several years, a mutt, cute
As early Disney, met the Trans-
Alpine Express and never missed
A one; he's ailing now but has
A protégé, scruffy as a swagman. Over
There, a surveyor was first to cross

The mountains. He had a dog, too but
Had to eat him.
For sale in the foothills are abandoned
Miners' shacks, cheaper than dinner for two
At the Auckland Yacht Club. Over the hump,
Down on the Canterbury Plain is a homestead
With lines of gaudy laundry; it's as if
The lady of the house has hung
Her stamp collection out to dry. Her
Party dress is Zanzibar, and Brazil
Her bustier.
Finally here's Christchurch
Where the pubs are packed
With McMurdo Station
Refugees. And
Along the Avon
She'll be waiting,
Maybe; just for me.

OASIS

Like a Tuareg desert camp,
Teredo Street coffee shop.
But no sand, date palms, nor
Dunes to hide denuded
Trees and gravel pit and belt.
Caravanserai of trades trucks.
Proud pick-ups. Inside large women
And salesmen. Posters celebrating
This ravaged landscape, landscape
Of what used to be. There's no
Turning back. An awkward eagle
Adorns office block. Custom
Carpet over ancestor bones.
Tribal council built Wiggiwa's
Discount smokes. Ads ask
Are your chakras in order, urge
Getting with past life regression.
Yes, take me way back
To us picking May mountain
Roses high on Tetrahedron.
First nomads a thousand
Years ago, here just south
Of the Reversing Falls.

TEN-IN-ONE

Carnival trucks with air-
Brushed clowns and tramps
And horizons. Three days sharing
The road, Cache Creek
To Hay River. Roughies,
Ride boys encountered
At service stations and pull-outs.

I envision the geek and the dwarf
Tumbling out of a trailer's rear door,
And the pinhead and the rubber man
Helping the giggling fat lady down.

The faded blue jeans guy with shades
And black t-shirt, grabbing eight
Cold ones at High Level. Dark-
Skinned amphetamine blond
Bouncing at his side eagerly grasping
His hard sunburned arm.

Me, the inconspicuous townie from
Some other town, watching
From beyond the coffee urns. He's
Playing me thirty years ago
And she could be you or
More likely some other one.

They're living a big romance
Begun at winter quarters
And taken on the road.
What are the odds they'll last
Until June's first tear-down?

I know the answer to that one
But still I watch, ever hopeful,
Ever deluded, as a Daumier dwarf
Spins the gaudy
Wheel of things.

MARY KATHLEEN

Mummy all sticks last visit.
Attached to tanks
Like a skeleton welder,
Hideous WW II Posada engraving
Of Rosie the Riveter in last days.
Mummy at Camp Lee outside
Office with other girls
In sundresses and Betty Boop shoes.
Big hair, like the shadow
Of a sycamore tree against
The old Dominion night. White
Smiles for a bright future and young men.
Grade school boyfriend Joseph Cotten long
Gone to Mercury Theatre and famous movies.
Coy look in black and white for one,
Exotic because his name ended
In a vowel; dangerous
Because from up north.

Hiroshima, Nagasaki and me
Brand new. First memory,
I must have been one and a half:
Watching from pillow-bounded bed
In Reese Street rowhouse as they
Wake, Mummy sitting up
Bare-breasted, smiling.
Another day same room, her
Taking me in arms to window
Saying, "Wave to daddy." Him
Looking up, sharp part in hair,
Smiling, in short sleeves. Two

Black kids rolling iron hoop
In the redbrick background. Me,
Dumb of arguments or unhappiness
For years. Most of that spent
On streets and summer fields.
Maybe forgetful or didn't hear or no
Room in young psyche until
Innocence-ending slap age five
In the narrow Catherine Street kitchen
In front of Aunt Adele. First
Of many I would remember.
In the suburbs they proliferated
Like TV antennas on roofs
In subdivisions of ugly split
Levels.
Slap slap.
Orders, demands, fights, constant
Critiques of homework and hair
And lawn-mowing.

Them fighting, me on the other
Side of a closed door with R & B radio.
Mummy and daddy accompanying
Sunnyland Slim.
Mummy being nice, talking baby talk
I knew at age eleven was crazy.
Mummy slap-slapping. The right hand
Giving it, and giving it again
On the way back while the left
Hand held the cigarette that
Wrinkled the squinting eye.

Them agreeing only over TV
Dinners – Salisbury steak Swanson

Hideous turkey in silver trays –
On one subject, hurling dark
Words over the table, like
Poker players, raising each
Other with epithets for
Dusky neighbours.

Oh, Mummy, nostalgic for the Southland
Of her girlhood and a South before
That. Meanwhile, Communists and Jew
Eggheads were trying to invade
Brookdale. She kept getting up
From chair to peer between
The blinds to see.
Finally, I got sent to the corner
Store for smokes and never came back.
Eventually went to Canada, and she
Insisted on moving to New Jersey
From shame over son, yet
Defended me in television interview.

Mummy, final visit
To New Jersey to see.
Last memory: moving her – she weighed
Nothing, but oxygen tanks were heavy –
From bed to living room.
Turned on television. She stared
At black people sit-com
And muttered during the fake laughter,
Papier-mâché flesh, and spoke
Through twisted mouth, "It's
Disgusting. Niggers! They
Want the things like what we got."
I sighed.

Half a century in that sigh
And she heard, turned, once radiant
Young girl Camp Lee face now
A death's head and spit
Last words on earth to her son,
Son who never made her proud,
Had amounted to nothing, "You
Always liked them, the niggers."
Finally, one moment's silent look
Of disgust, before
Dismissing me from her life.

And she died a month later, buried
In Blandford Cemetery adjacent to
Petersburg Monument Battlefield
Park. The birth date in stone engraved
Strange to me. Years older
Than she always claimed.
My mother, Mary Kathleen,
Mummy.

AT THE POET'S PLACE

The stairs bear hieroglyphs
From the classic drinking period, like
A steep grey lawn when somebody
Didn't remove the garden hose
Through a week of sun and rain.
The corridors are empty of Annies.
The genius gone east to be awarded.
Me, seated on wino couch,
And everywhere, the poet
Can stare across the room
At himself. The chairs are all
On a bender like wobbly loggers
And what's behind that cabinet's
Duct taped door? Closet
Bulging with comic books like Clark
Kent grown too big for his booth.
You could draw Faux-Pas Man
With your finger on the dinner plates.
A tower of caps like MG drivers wear.
On the spare room's bed, sheets
That haven't been changed since Nutter
Died. His old man's blood still low down
On the wall like a midget's abstract
Expressionism. The CDs neat in their rack
Like ash drawers in a Necropolis. No
Apricot air in here. I batter
The windows open, a bird comes
To the sill and wind ruffles
Press clippings as I scrub
The genius's floor.

AT THE INTERSECTION

After all shawarmas have been eaten
And mochaccinos memories. When
Streetcars melt and great
Grandchildren of babushka widows younger
Than me have been obliterated. After
The Forever Beauty and Health Spa, O
Buzio restaurant and Banco Espiritu
Are never more and each of their minimum
Wage workers meet always untimely but
Oh-so-predictable fates – in other
Words, after the ball is over,
After the morons in charge, brothers all
In jelaba, burnoose or rep tie
Have choked us to death with hands white,
Black, yellow or brown, and blown us each
And everyone to smithereens,
Not even affording
The opportunity of following
That fado float out of here, capering
To mandolins, the dance of happy shades
Through the metaphorical curtain
To the metaphorical other side –
After all that,
Will there be someone
Or anything to remember or conjure
What might once have been, as I
On variety store stoop see
A frog pond world of before
When a redcoat wandered up from
The shore of a sweet water lake,
And two Indians enveloped

In four arms and four legs spied
Under a catalpa tree on a dragon fly
Day like this is, while the tall grass
Undulated as if from a migration
Of writhing souls?

SOAKING WET GIRL

Late at night, a knocking at my
Trailer door. You stand dripping
On the threshold, short black hair
Like a shower cap, and shining
In the porch light. Windbreaker stuck
To your body. I didn't recognize you,
Having only met you that one time
At your parents' house.
You're eighteen and I'm considerably
Older than they.

The other girls didn't wait for you
After the dance, left you stranded
In the parking lot. No buses running.
Two miles you walked through the rain
To here. Your accent is charming. I can't
Turn you away. Your runners squeak as you
Come in. I give you towels and a black silk
Robe that someone gave me, and I've worn
Only once.

When you come out of the washroom, I say
That a glowing fireplace would be just the thing
But I only have this oven to sit before.
You stretch your legs, orange heels and soles
On the edge of the door. When I see you glance
A second time at the bottle of Demerara rum
I ask if you'd like a glass
And you say, "Yes, please." All shy,
Or are you acting shy? I admit
To being a little afraid, no acting.

Half the bottom half of the robe,
By the middle of your second drink,
Opens like a black orchid's errant
petal. "I'm warm now," you say,
As we consider the elements.

You talk about the old country, and things
Being so different here, and then you sigh
And say that you suppose
Your clothes won't be dry until the morning.

SASKATCHEWAN SUMMER

Stepped down from the train
With the corn fed girl, come back
From the eastern city,
And shook the mother's hand, like a small
Work glove. The girl sat up front
In the Crown Victoria, hair defiant strands
Of golden tall grass prairie outside open windows
As we rolled south of Weyburn.

But home now, longing for the old farm,
She'd defy no more. The mother
Forty-two years old, husband gone
From diabetes, a decade nearly.
There were seasonal men and a lead hand
Who stared at the daughter's tall, strong body
Wondering what new knowledge of it she might
Have acquired back there where men
Stay up all night long.

There was a cot for me in a corner of the barn
And I'd have to work for my keep.
But that was fine by me, assuming
The mother kept her own counsel
And to her accounts when the dishes were done.

We took moonlight walks, the corn fed
Girl and I, half a mile to the mailbox,
Holding hands, wrapped
In the smell of wheat and grey
Earth, wildflowers and the night.
Her golden body, taut-armed, high-breasted,

Cheek bones sharp, gentian eyes.
But we'd only kiss before she'd shrug away
Anticipating what might come next
And maybe saving me embarrassment.

I'd walk back, kicking clumps, to the barn,
Wanting to think the stars were mocking me
Lacklove on the prairie, so close I might
Have poked them out, one by one
And might still be at it, 40-odd years later,
Grandfather three or four times over, still
Running the farm. My hair and that
Of the corn fed girl like hoarfrost
On the Thanksgiving fields. But
One night, hands under head, motionless
On the bunk arranged just so,
So the quarter moon
Had its own quarter panel of window
At which I gazed, there was a determined
Rapping on the door and, of course,
It was the mother, barefoot
In a slip that smelled of mothballs,
Stale perfume at the backs of her knees
And the tops of her thighs. Every night
For a week her rough hands were all over
My body and we spent hours as if there
Were no such thing as chores, no seasons
Only flesh and moist and limbs to tangle.
And that's how the lead hand found us
When the sun was long up, twisted
In sleep like the ropes in another corner
Of the barn. And crashing around,
Woke us and saw his boss's thighs
As she swung them off the cot,

And breasts like small animals
Moved in rose-faded satin.
Later he took a swing at me
And missed, fell in the dirt of the barnyard
And cried, big hands before his face,
Figuring plans, sown so many seasons past
Had been killed by this ill-weather from the east.
The daughter spoke neither to me nor her mother,
And it was time to leave. So
Alone this time I made the mailbox walk,
Then went south on the 35. I refused
The offer of a ride, and another. Turned west
On 13 and kept refusing, and walked
All the way across Saskatchewan
That callow, decades' gone, green summer
Turned sentimental and golden
Now in late Autumn.

IN RESPONSE TO THE WOMAN I HADN'T SEEN IN NEARLY THIRTY YEARS WHO INFORMED ME THAT I PROBABLY WOULD HAVE MADE IT INTO "CANADIAN LITERATURE" HAD I NOT WASTED MY YOUTH AND EARLY MANHOOD

Yes, when I was a boy, I was
A busboy, delivery boy,
Stock boy. And it was often,
"Hey, boy!"
A few years later, I was a
Shipper-receiver, carnie
Deceiver, a soda jerker,
Construction worker, nail-
Banger and I even cleaned up
An airplane hangar.
Yes, and then I became a man:
A delivery man, stock man,
Lead hand and managed a band.
I worked in a laundry, a library,
Picked cherries,
Avocados, corn too,
Row after row, was a census taker
Leaves raker, lawn mower,
Seed sower.
And did hundreds of other things.
All the time hitching and hopping
On and off buses,
Careening ocean to ocean
Like one of those silly toys
Bumping into boardwalks
And crossing the country all over again.

All the time though I read and
Knowing no better began
With the usual but that didn't work
So I turned to other things.
At lunch breaks on loading ramps,
Hanging by a subway strap.
On nighttime Trailways my light
Was the only one on as we crossed cold
Wyomings. I hid out in skid row rooms
With Jack London.
And I got the news
Not from Papa but Langston Hughes.
Found Chester Himes, Richard Wright,
Willard Motley in three-for-a-quarter
Backstreet bins. Southern
And Midwestern libraries
Were like lunch counters,
And their kind wasn't served.
I read *The Big Clock, The Big Cage,*
Kenneth Fearing, Robert Lowry,
Who knows them anymore?
Rechy and Selby and Jack and Allen.
Mostly though it was certain Frenchmen.
Carco kept me company.
I heard "The Ballad of a Hanged Man"
In the Sioux Falls jail but it was a hobo
Who sprung me, not a king. In
Detroit and Louisville, I ran into
Robinson. Hopping a freight
Out of East St. Louis, I found Moravagine,
Twisted up on the straw in the corner
His lips smeared with blood.
Perhaps it meant something
And perhaps it didn't, all of that.

Maybe you're right and I should
Have gotten with a university
And burrowed in but what
Would those decades have been
Like? It doesn't matter. What does
Is that, wandering boy I may have been
And mixed-up man but I wouldn't
Trade any of it – what I read,
What I sought and did –
For what you say I ought. No,
Not for all the world because
I had the world and have it still
But thanks for your opinion
And fuck you, too.

FOREVER MARIA

Just throw my junk out the window,
Baby. It's of no use to me anymore.
None of it's worth a good goddamn
And I can't face coming round. You'd
Just tear a strip off my hide
Make fun of my haircut and my
Twenty-year old car, this
Secondhand sport coat, our third-
Rate romance. How could you ever
Have gotten involved
With the sorry-ass likes of me?

The red suit and yellow wing-
Tip slip-ons? I was never
Cut out to be a pimp or an Elk.
That glow-in-the-dark Virgin
Of Guadalupe? All she ever did
Was light the way from your bed
To the shelf that held the booze.
And I never had the nerve
To wear those shirts from Samoa.
Out with the Jim Tully stories, nobody
Cares about them or this shanty Irish,
Circus boy either.

As for the Billie Holiday sides,
Give them the old heave-ho. It
Ain't nobody's business
What you do, as if you ever cared.
Throw it all out the window.
Let the junkman have it, or maybe
You already did.

Just mail me that bus station photo.
The one where the beautiful young woman
Doesn't look too terribly upset
At being with the future no good
Worthless son-of-a-bitch who's
Squeezing her close,
There in Saskatoon.
She's in profile, smiling up at him,
Hoop earring a dangling blur
That's keeping count
Of the time that's running away.
You know the picture, the one
On the back of which, in purple ink,
Is written: Your baby forever,
Maria.

On second thought, throw that
Out the window first of all,
Baby.

CAPE FEAR

Darling, Sarracenia, I found
You amongst bog and rocky
Outcroppings, struck dumb
That such glory flowered
In a meager soil. You stood
Alone, no neighbours, neither
Rose nor nasturtium for those
Were not the bougainvillea
Lands. A stranger to your
Parts, I learned you succeed
Where others perish. Unaware
Of your pitfall traps, I would
Tumble to all of them.
When you vowed to digest me, I
Thought it fancy talk. You
Showed the operculum covering your
Opening, and I entered like a pilgrim,
A penitent, a prisoner long without,
And reveled in the mucilage. Who
Could have resisted when from
Your peristope nectar flowed. And
I was trapped. That
Sweetness being coniine, same
Found in hemlock.
And the way out sealed
By thorns and tendrils.

DEAD OR OTHERWISE

Well, Phil, three months
Now ashes in a pewter urn you'd
Never have on your mantle
Piece. Ninety-four days exactly
Doing what dead spirits
Supposed to do. What's that? As
Good as boulevardiering? Our gothic
Walks, you splay-legged, long arms
Windmilling, me to the side
And a step behind
To keep out of danger? Walks to
Look at gables and lintels, friezes
And crooked porches? No more country
Music or gossip. Does spirit world
Have substitutes for, say,
The skyline of books around
Your sofa or legs of Czech film
Editor? Is there indeed anything,
Dead or otherwise, where you are? Where
Are you? Let me know, Philguy, friend
Of thirty-four years, please, and
Forthwith.

VIRGIN OF JUQUILA

Under the sun and various palms.
Behind the yellow-bordered image,
A bass drum, and brass flattened
By the hot wind. With black slacks
And skirts, the white-shirted procession
Flanked by a pair of serious dogs.
In the last line, two men support
The elbow sticks of the brown widow
Who'd been a beauty
In the Pancho Villa time.

Here the last palm, date
Palm, brilliant in the yard
And sky. Magnificent fronds
Making their own music,
Sounding like rain, like dry
Leaves on a broken pavement,
Like aces and eights in bicycle
Spokes; fronds like the virgin's
Many arms in green silk,
Elegant fingertips brushing
The lid of the casket, laid
Out on trestles below.

SUSPICIOUS BEHAVIOUR

The skinny black trucker asked me to take the wheel.
And, reaching over the two shift levers, I sighted down
The long Peterbilt hood, thinking he was going
For a thermos or making adjustments or
Unsticking his pants from the seat.
But when one black hand was back on the wheel,
The tops of his green, heavy-duty working man's pants
Were halfway to his knees. I saw pale blue satin johnsons
With lace trim, his equipment like rugged country
    underneath,
And he, left handedly, began wailing away at his member,
"Oh, yeah! Ride me, papa. Ride me, papa!"

I looked straight down the hood at six lanes
Of 5 P.M. traffic, and out the side window
At mini-malls and factory outlet stores
Flashing by like junk mail.
"Whack, whack. Satin-wrapped!" exclaimed the driver,
As Joe Tex on the radio finished
Singing about Skinny Legs and a third voice
Said, "Now, over to Jim in the Whirlibird
With the WXOX traffic report."
"Thank you, Bob. Traffic's moving smoothly
On I-77, along the Canton-Akron corridor, except,
That is, for one old Peterbilt conventional."
"What seems to be the problem, Jim?"
"Well, Bob, it appears the driver is abusing himself..."
"Abusing himself? You mean...?"
"That's exactly what I mean, Bob. Right there
In front of God and six lanes of rush hour traffic
And he's not alone."

"You mean, there're two self-abusers?"
"No, the passenger's pretending not to notice As the truck
    begins to lurch and jolt, like, if you'll
Pardon the expression, a kangaroo..."
"A kangaroo, Jim?"
"That's right, Bob. A kangaroo trying to get
To the outhouse with a broken leg."
"Very metaphorical or picturesque, or whatever
The hell it is, Jim."
"Thanks again, Bob. Now let me just add
That this kind of activity is definitely a traffic hazard,
You have to do something like that, pull over.
Pull over at a rest stop."
"Jim, you mean, pull over if you have to pull it out,
Sort of thing." "Yes, thanks for the slogan, Bob. Folks,
Think of your fellow drivers or your passenger,
For heaven's sake."

The truck bucked to a halt
And stalled there in the curb lane.
The skinny black driver, wiping his left hand
On his green pants, johnsons stained dark blue, saying,
"That was some ride, say what, Whitey?"
As I jumped down.
He got it started and lurched away just as a highway
Patrol cruiser pulled up. The guy got out, gun drawn,
Pointed it at me, said, "Don't you know
There's a law against hitchhiking on the Interstate?
You look suspicious, boy. I'm gonna have to
Take you in." And I said,
"But, but..."

MARIMBA FOREVER

Four on the Alameda
By the Cathedral's south
Side door, rigid like figures
In an architect's rendering,
Heads turned from the glittering apse
As in the engraving of 1552,
To survey the zocalo scene.
And were watching when the first
Package tour tourists arrived
From north of the border, seeking
Brown skin and syncopated music.
It is said Cortez tripped
Over a cobblestone, exactly
Forty-one paces from the bandstand stairs,
And nuzzled Malinche's neck
On that green bench
Right over there where
I wish I were necking with you.
Conquistadors in armour sat before marble-
Topped tables, sipping chocolate how many
Dead Indians ago? And
Touched their morions when a pretty
Zacateca girl went swishing by.
Same tables hustled by how many
Generations of guitar players?
And how many, like him,
Were missing a string, singing
"Bessa Me Mucho" but much
Too dirty ever to kiss, and
Oblivious to marimba orchestra
Making background music to
Tomorrow's memories.

MIRACLE AT SEVEN PERSONS

Just south of Medicine Hat, north of Burdett
On the gravel shoulder in the arid lands
Pointed west, old four-door Caddy
PEI plates and its hood up as if
In surrender. In passenger seat, dirty-face
Girl on a lap wide enough for these open spaces
Another hefty woman, somebody's mother-in-law
In the back with twin boy toddlers
And an older, cross-eyed kid.
A gaunt, lank-haired man stares bewildered
At an engine compartment that resembles
The badlands up ahead, as steam rises
From the canyon floor.
A tableau of seven travelers near the old Turkey Track
And the creek where the Great Spirit smote another
Seven in the early times. Me and pronghorn
Sheep take a long view of this. What're the odds
Of these back east refugees making
The evergreen coast?

Suddenly
In the piebald sky appears
The angel of mercy who smiles,
Radiant above a gown of voluminous white.
Young and comely enough to never
Sit out a dance in roadhouses hereabouts.
Fortunately, I remembered this time
To bring my camera and have recorded
The miracle forever, having missed
So many in the past.

SHANNON FALLS

You told me all the women
I write about are schemers
And run-arounds, that
I must never have known
The love of a bright-eyed, non-
Neurotic. But you are wrong.

Her name was Shannon and she
Had a sunny disposition that
Never acknowledged the rain.
She was big for in-line skating
And prided herself in thinking
Outside the box. "I bet you
Push the envelope, too," I
Said. "Oh, I do," she replied,
Sipping her one drink
Of the evening. It had
More umbrellas sticking out
Of it than a café in Cancun.

See, I thought it was more than time
For a change; I'd spring-clean my
Personal house of tawdry horrors, stick
A happy face on what I liked to call
My love life. She wore sports bras,
And got waxed every Wednesday.
Her body looked airbrushed; she'd
Taken a course in realizing sexual
Fulfillment, from a woman who looked
Like Mahatma Gandhi.
My friends envied me but I dreaded

Those evenings after ananga ranga
Afternoons, down in our cups, or my
Cups. She never talked about death,
Always changed the subject
To Ikea. Me, I've always liked them
With a wreath for a smile and imagine
Their faces behind long, black veils when
They visit my grave after I've been
Murdered by someone their
Husbands hired.

We'd go hiking, and she posed
On every promontory to exclaim over
The beauty of it all, as if she'd had
Something to do with it.

And there we were halfway down
The road from Whistler, one Sunday
Afternoon après ski, at Shannon
Falls where we stopped to "Oooh"
And "Aaah," full of health, and plans
To climb the face of the Squamish Chief.
Whatever. Of course, I must have
Thought of it in advance, given
The symmetry, as if I'd known
The day of reckoning was nigh. I'd
Been stalling about my portfolio, all
Full, I'd said, of eco-friendly investments,
Just like hers.
The water
Was booming and roiling, and...
And I just pushed.
Over the edge she went
And for a moment seemed

Suspended like a cartoon character
Flailing in Lycra with paradise
For a backdrop.

So I headed south to North Van,
And at the old Centennial met a woman
With a crooked mouth and three
Ex-husbands and teeth chipped
Like the red, day-before-yesterday
Polish on her toenails. After last call, we
Went back to her place and drank
Rye whiskey, messed around and fell
Asleep with the lights on. She
Was afraid Death
Would come creeping
In the dark.

WILD WEST DAYS

Holed up in the bowling alley basement
Courtesy of our co-conspirator, the owner
With hairy fingers who claimed not
To give a shit about young love or anything
Else save Graziano and Marciano
And Joey Giardello. Hearing the hoofs
Of the posse in the alley, we smooched,
Theresa and I, and schemed until
Noon when we'd be inconspicuous
On streets of lunchtime children.
Over Wolfe, back to Ritner, down
To Porter, across the wide Oregon
To rows of battered behemoths,
Cars like bulbous couches, a million
Lustrous ideals now pitted like old bumper-
Chrome, a million dreams
Down on their rims.

But what did we know, street urchins,
Age eleven? Smack
Dab in the middle was that patch
Of hard earth flatter than Death
Valley's floor, and horse hair and horse
Sweat vanished all oil refinery stink.
Two horses, not nags too old
For the ice wagon with backs
That sagged like hammocks, but
Mustangs only half-broken,
Like Gene and Roy's, and sotto
Voce we called them Champion
And Trigger, remembering how

The Negro'd laughed when first
He'd heard us. This was not
A piece of junkyard enclosed
By a fence of automobile hoods
And trunks but wide open spaces
With hoodoos and crevasses just west
Of west Texas, not the extreme south
Of South Philadelphia. There were
Even real gunshots for verisimilitude.
We climbed into the saddle, the wind
From Oregon Avenue blew through
Your tangled Italian mane, skirts
Half up your coltish legs, and we
Rode off into the afternoon's
Setting sun, reading signs of unshod
Indian ponies in patterns of spilled
Crankcase oil. Headed for the border,
We adlibbed lines of this dada western.

The Negro's head lolled back to catch
The sun or washed his hands over
An oilcan fire, humming Jack McVey
Solos maybe while we galloped through
The long shadows out where a friend
Is a friend.

They came and got me, Theresa while
You slept with your feet to the fire
Under a canopy of stars, our horses
Hobbled in the wild flowers. I kissed
Your lips that smelled of sage
And oregano. My parents
Made me go in a Buick.

It was years before I broke free
And headed west. I really did
Work on a ranch. It was in Nevada.
And I rode a horse in a Mexican movie.
Did you stay an outlaw cowgirl, break
Hearts in dance halls or marry a guy
From the neighbourhood, have
Six kids like a good girl whose roots
Reached to the other side? I've thought
Of you in many a saloon, waited
For you to come down the stairs
In fishnets and spangles.

Were any two kids as crazy
And in love, Theresa, as we were
On stolen afternoons
Of our Wild West days?

REAL LOVE

The clapboard cottage
At the rainforest edge
Trembling on pilings, the inlet
A water colour drop seeping
Over the porch rail. First evening,
Dinner dishes pushed to the centre,
Chairs pushed back, your
Bare knees pointed at me, I parted
Them and got on my own, finally
After awkward teasing in the junkyard
And those gypo camp kisses, parted
Them and ran tongue along insides
Of warm thighs getting warmer. Your
Thick hair then, then your taste,
The wetness. I wanted to drink
It all, and wanted it all over me,
But finally drew you to your
Feet, kissed the beauty mark at
The bridge of your nose
And to the left. Then you understood
My hands gentle tug and turned
As I lifted the bottom
Of your dress – cotton, summer,
Flower-faded – and you bent
Forward from the waist. So
Beautiful, I stood back
To better see, legs perfect
Columns, smooth, honey. Spine
Dipped, rear rose to me.
I entered you then first time
And was gone. And I knew

It sliding in. Gone,
As you are gone
From me now far away
And I can only sit here,
Remembering.

MY BUDDY

He's always there. But
Hangs back, usually. So I
Forget all about him or
Pay him little mind, most
Of the time. Oh, maybe
At four in the morning
He rolls them bones
On the tin roof, gives
Me a nudge, a wink, a
Bit of a fright. Then I
Forget about him again, like
Breathing. Sometimes
Looking back, I'm amazed
By his tact. He didn't
Rub it in when she was found
In the gutter beaten and dead
And funny how he stayed
Out of the Cartagena dungeon. I'd
Have thought he'd be
In his element but I was young
And didn't know him well.
My buddy's on the bus, winking
With the eyes of the console Buddha.
From the rearview mirror, dangling,
Batting coy Virgin of Guadalupe lashes.
My buddy's really always everywhere
Just biding his time. It's his
Time after all.
With me he turns mean
When it gets wild. When
It gets good. He was there

In the highlands when
I looked for the big animals. And
Peeked from behind
The jungle's golden Madonna.
Now it's the flat, cold chisel stare.
He's in the sidecar; the wind's
In my hair, lips bared, music
In my head, when
He makes a grab
For the suicide shift, but he's not
Quick enough because he
Doesn't want to be quick enough.
Not yet.
Walking along the two-lane
Winding road, shirt open
To the sun's caress, a kid
On a water buffalo smiles. It's then
My buddy appears, out of the long grass
"Nice isn't it?" he asks, and answers:
"No, it's perfect! Yes, indeed. Always
Have been days like this. Always
Will be.
Always."

SOUTH CHINA SEA

The South China Sea through a cycad screen.
Fishing boats like gnats and a dragon fly
Of a freighter. On the sand at six
As picturesque as you'd wish.
A dark kid coiling rope among the dawn's
Dead jelly fish. Now
There's only me and a woman in satin
Pink pajamas sweeping sand.
Rhythm of her broom,
Harmony of waves. In back of me
Dunes and a Cham temple.
Four hours down the road
Sai Gon like a whore with
Scuffed shoes and dirty
Knees.

WATER TRAFFIC

Kids at the water park, giggling
On the slides, laughing
In a wave pool, yelling
Somewhere on the crazy
River.

Young parents and grandmothers in the shade
Guarding knapsacks and picnic snacks. Others
Under the frond woven roof of a bar
On pilings over the real
Mudbank river. The detritus of jungle
Rushing by on a brown current, as if eager
To become islands. Stolid barges
And tugs like old draught horses;
Flaking-paint scows with mysterious
Prow symbols in fresh vermillion.

Just over there, mines popped out
The port side of the Baton Rouge
That I wasn't on. The two men
At the tin table, one one-armed,
Were also twenty-one or twenty-two that year.
They're playing a tabletop game
With caps from all the BGIs
They drank today.

Brown water between gaps in foot-wide
Floor boards appears to be hiding
From rain that now patters
The river out there
Like desultory rifle fire.

The inevitable available girl,
Shaking her top foot, toes
Jiggling a white shoe, is perched
On the dragon edge of the corn plant.
Bare arms and bare legs, barely older
Than water-park kids, and as old
As the river traffic. And now thunder
Rumbles like a distant barrage.

ADIOS, AMIGO

Last night as I read your note.
It occurred to me, you'll not
Be around for any reply. Your final one,
And first without an alias. I realized too,
The central diamond-clear image
Of you: not behind the wheel,
Me riding shotgun with a copper
Rockethead load. Nor you like a cowboy
On the alien city campus. Or in court-
Room chains or a thousand other facets
Of our mad careening. No, it's
A North Carolina day job. We jumped
Down from the big Reo in Rocky Mount
And I ran across the 301, got us hired.
You hauling lumber. Me pushing barrows.
I stopped at the top of a ramp
To swipe at my forehead with the back
Of a hand and looked across the site
Like a Golden Book illustration: the foreman
Explaining blueprints in a Hieronymous
Bosch hat. The Caterpillar was a dinosaur.
The dump truck, a squat acrobat
Doing its one trick. And over by the lumber pile
The slim, blond Errol Flynn-desperado-looking guy
Looking back. You waved; I waved. Your Indian
Eyes saying, "Let's get our pay and get back
On that highway. I've never been
To New York City."
My first great friend, eager for it all
In 1965. Mad for a big life. Nearly
Forty years later now, at the end

Of it, in hospital bed, chicken peck
Scrawl note bids
Adios, Amigo.

ALL GET OUT

Dawn's slipping over the hillock
Like a bashful angel in gaudy
Clothes. It reminds
Me of you in that way.
Those are not my apollonia trees.
Who even has
Wallpaper these days? That buttock
I reach behind to touch. Is
It yours? It better be.
I remember now. The moon
Last night was a silver hammock
That swayed when I wasn't looking
And broadcast a Milky Way.
I was distracted. I like to fancy
The satin sheets are ripped
And ruined and resemble the dawn
That just now is fading.
"Too bad night turns to dawn
And both have to go away
Forever, just like you," you say.
Adding that it has to be this way.
"If you stay I don't know what
I might do. I can't be responsible. I just
Don't trust myself."

I suppose you want
Me to call your bluff. Then
You'll have someone
To blame whatever it is on.
I should have learned that by now.
Ripped slips, broken heels, merlot

On the carpet, stockings
With ladders and potatoes. And, oh,
The screams. Under our feet
The knob end of the broom
Of the downstairs neighbour.
And maybe this morning,
Flowers, blooming outside the door
From the Mexican in Fifth Business.
Now that I know the game
I can throw in my hand.
I'll slip into my slip-ons
And slip out, grab my grip
As the day slips in after me,
And you pretend to sleep
Watching me go. And the door
Closes like a prison cell. It's
Romantic as all get-out. And
The flowers are there, too.
Mock orange.

THE BIG NOWHERE

I made a movie in my head,
Even drove the crafts' truck, did the sets,
The casting too. But I brought in Wally
Westmore to tame your face. No
Audience would ever believe such
Savage beauty. You were the Femme
Fatale. It was a B-flick, of course.
Veronica Lake had nothing on you. Linda
Darnell was a wistful panther
In a faded slip as you walked
Out of the Big House. "You'll
Be back," she muttered. You were Ida
Lupino playing piano in that roadhouse.
But Richard Widmark tried to scare
The wrong guy, see. You were Gloria
Grahame, and I pistol-whipped Lee
For that stunt with the coffee pot.
Your nails and lips were Chinese
Lacquer. Dresses cut on the bias. Sure
You had a past and a husband trapped
In Surabaya. It was messy but I
Got him out and we sent him
Packing. Trouble was
I wouldn't throw the championship.
And it had to end badly:
Me, the blind newsboy
Lolling my head and listening
On a cathedral radio
As my brother played Carnegie Hall.
And I went back, punchy,
To a four-bit room, tap

Tapping my cane, while at the end
Of South Street, your bus pulled out
Into a thick mist, headed
For the Big Nowhere.

SINGAPORE BLUES

I'm in Singapore in a courtyard,
Waiting. The building surrounds
Me like a noose. Noon's fierce
Sun is a searchlight
And I walk the shade
Perimeter, like an inmate
Let out for exercise, or
A shy player reluctant
To take centre stage or
A guy with a lot to hide.
And the building spins
And the world turns
And the face in your window
Looking down at me
Will change, and someone
Take my place, too, walking
Round and round.

HE'S NOT DRUNK

Sipping Sols on the corner
In that tropical town of ships,
And palms and laughing girls.
Riding across the night through
Agave shadows, passing the bottle
And the tales. That old
Man in the Guatemala mountains,
Withered, with a scythe, and
Wreathed in sycamore smoke.
We both recognized him
And dared to laugh.
And had another one.

Hey, and down the road now
There just went Murphy. But, he
Wasn't drunk,

                    he

                              just

                                        stumbled

Into the usual

                    great

                              big

                                        bunch

                                                  of

                                                            Nothing.

And of his raucous passing, left
A blood red reminder
All over the white
Escondido wall.

AN OLDIE BUT A GOODY

It's five A.M. and this one's
Going out to all those who just
Kicked off the dark blanket
Of a night that tried to smother them,
Whose eyes weren't blinded
By the street's false glitter, or stars
That lucky ones wish upon
And their dreams came true.
Just imagine that...

To those who toughed it out
Through wee small hours
With a pint
And a pack of smokes and Sinatra,
With Al Green or Lester.
Yeah, this one's especially
Dedicated to Marcel and Lorraine
Down on Howland Avenue, the
Ashes will turn to fire next time.
And it's also going out to Linda H.
Get out of that gutter, girl.
The light of dawn's going
To spread and cauterize your wounds,
And you'll cross your Rio
Bravo, one more time.
And it's for Floyd and Liberal
Earl and Emma J. who never
Got out of Wangerei, and to
JFD Junior who did his time,
A dime, and called his ass
His own. To Luscious Louise,
Six foot-five and a stand up guy.

Yes, it's going out to the peek
Freaks who just can't help it. Old
Gus Dundebeggar, the cop
On the beat and any old time Pete
Man who never met a box
He couldn't peel. To the lady
In the crummy in Truckee
And the woman with no arms, and
Silver satin panties in the Howard
Johnson's in Arlington, Virginia.
To Billy, the kid with a tail.
And Shelley and Keats, and Duncan
Reynaldo, to has-been's
Never was's and ain't gonna be's. To
Everyone all around the water tower
Waiting for a train.

To all those strangers
Who put a light on
In all those houses that stand
Alone on prairies and badlands
Spread across a black night
From Siberia to Saskatoon.
To everybody waiting
For the early edition to reach
The corner boxes.

Yes, this song's dedicated to you
And all the ones I didn't mention.
You know who you are. It's
And oldie but a goody, and I just
Realized, it's been around the station
Forever. It's got catchy lyrics
And a rhumba beat. It's a little

Thing called: "You Can Bet Your Ass,
Things Ain't Never
Gonna Change."
I hope you like it...

AUTO-BIOGRAPHY

I wanted to see old broke cars.
Especially round ones like Edwardian
Sofas, with side-view mirrors
Dangling like arthritic hands.
There I am at four,
Excited in the back seat. Parents
In front, pleased their kid
Needs no amusement parks,
Ice cream cones. The 1939
Plymouth long landfill under Philadelphia
Airport runway. Parents long ashes both.
Me, awed, laughing, pointing
At comic Studebakers like camels
Resting on their axles, rusted, broken-
Tooth grilles grinning back.
A Kaiser-Fraser with one sun visor
Turned down like a man who'd
Shaved off an eyebrow.
Old broke cars with running boards
For the little tramp to jump upon
And steal a ride, and him and it
To ass-and-tea kettle clatter
Down the long road
From there
To here.

MISSING MY MISSING ON ALL THE AVENIDAS

Trees in the park of San Martin
Are twisted and black like the hands
Of a bluesman too arthritic to play
His own relief and for surcease
From a haunting face but, me, I
Need to consult old photos to remember
Exactly how you look.

There used to be tango on Corrientes.
Now it's rarer than you in Buenos Aires.
But I found one place, Café Eye
De Ahl, and thought of you
Who used to be my ideal. Closer
Than lianas entwined,
We might have had
The same milk mother.

Now, it's Bogota again, after
Thirty years and the same number
Of governments, and I almost long
For the power you used to wield.
The coke fiend ambassador lost
His mind, half his nose and both
Epaulets. His gypsy mistress,
Who wouldn't tell my future,
Is an ironing lady in the Czech Republic.
The octoroon's an octogenarian
But claims to have sold her favours
At the Tequendoma little more
Than a decade ago. Here I formerly
Missed someone else just as I did

You. Oh, break my heart
With tango songs from
Yesteryear, just like Gardel
Would do. Play the blues
San Martin trees:

    I got a hurt
    Oh, yeah I got a hurt
    But it don't have a face no more...

And I'm missing my missing
On all the Avenidas.

Buenos Aires–Bogota, December, 2007

WHY WE'RE IN AFGHANISTAN

Stevo cut down by small arms fire
And John fell into a well. Two Captains
Dead in one Afghanistan week
And "a major lost both his legs."

A piper of the Princess Pats
Played as their peers
Put them on the plane. And
A better ramp ceremony you
Never did see and you'll see
Plenty more.

But what of that major and his legs?
Where did he lose them? Or did
He step on a mine? The details
Don't matter only
That he lost them –
Doing his duty, that was.

Those fellows on the tarmac
All looked solemn, determined
And young. Maybe they'll live
To get stoned again
Come Saturday night, and even
Survive their tour, go back
To Creemore and Elkhorn
100 Mile House and Trois Rivières
Where they'll wake up some morning
A score and a-half years from now
And wonder what the hell was
Going on in that godforsaken place
Over there when they were young.

Sure, there're more than a few that
Made it, though some like Stevo
and Jon are dead, but what about
The other fellow? Will he too always be,
Like the Brigadier General said, "In
The thoughts and prayers
Of the entire Canadian Task Force,"
Or just "Old what-was-his-name
That good-looking fellow, 'a major
Who lost both his legs.'"
Is he back home with a generous
Compensation package and a couple
Of belt-on legs? Or maybe a rollerboard,
The plastic-covered titanium, state
Of the art number that comes with
The lightweight rubber blocks – individually
Contoured to fit your hands – all
The better to push himself about
And slide underneath automobiles
And fix
The Universal problem.

Could be he's doing push-ups
For beers right now in the pub
Back home. That girl he was
Slated to marry, is she
Still by his side, looking
Down on him?

Bet his legs even now are calling
Him but from heaven knows
Where. Are they with the Captain
Down at the bottom of the well?
Did someone throw them

To the dogs of Kandahar? Or
Did dusky kids play football
With his feet? Maybe they
Just up and walked away, his
Legs, over mountains
And through poppy fields
And are right now relaxing
In a room in Peshawar. Or

Maybe they're up in the sky,
And make constellations
Like a billion other limbs
From a million other wars.